Jean May

chicken

simple and delicious easy-to-make recipes

This is a Parragon Publishing Book
This edition published in 2004

Parragon Publishing
Queen Street House
4 Queen Street
Bath, BA1 1HE, UK

ISBN: 1-40543-858-4

Printed in China

Produced by
THE BRIDGEWATER BOOK COMPANY LTD

Photographer Calvey Taylor-Haw
Home Economist Ruth Pollock

Cover Photography Mark Wood
Home Economist Pamela Gwyther

NOTES FOR THE READER

- This book uses both imperial and metric measurements. Follow the same units of measurement throughout; do not mix imperial and metric.

- All spoon measurements are level: teaspoons are assumed to be 5 ml, and tablespoons are assumed to be 15 ml.

- Unless otherwise stated, milk is assumed to be whole milk, eggs and individual vegetables such as potatoes are medium, and pepper is freshly ground black pepper.

- Recipes using raw or very lightly cooked eggs should be avoided by infants, the elderly, pregnant women, convalescents, and anyone suffering from an illness.

- The times given are an approximate guide only. Preparation times differ according to the techniques used by different people and the cooking times may also vary from those given. Optional ingredients, variations, or serving suggestions have not been included in the calculations.

contents

introduction

Chicken is marvelously versatile and its popularity never seems to wane. From succulent appetizers and snacks to full traditional roast meals, this delicately flavored bird can provide a host of tantalizing dishes for every occasion. Whether that occasion is a simple lunch or an extravagant dinner party, a buffet, barbecue grill, picnic, or supper, the practical yet delicious versatility of chicken will always come into its own.

For the health-conscious among you, chicken is amazingly low in fat, especially when cooked without the skin. It is also extremely nutritious. Chicken is rich in protein and B vitamins, especially vitamin B3, which promotes healthy skin and digestion, boosts energy, and helps to lower cholesterol. Chicken is also an excellent source of magnesium, which helps to fight stress and depression and protects against heart attacks.

thai chicken soup
page 8

chicken with creamy spaghetti
page 42

On the flavor front, chicken combines well with so many delicious foods that the possible combinations are endless. It is also inexpensive, and a little can go a long way.

So what better way to capitalize on the marvelous benefits of chicken than by sampling the recipes in this book? Whatever the occasion, there is bound to be something in the following pages to suit every taste and every budget.

easy

Recipes are graded as follows:
1 spoon = easy;
2 spoons = very easy;
3 spoons = extremely easy.

serves 4

Recipes generally serve four people. Simply halve the ingredients to serve two, taking care not to mix imperial and metric measurements.

10 minutes

Preparation time. Where marinating or soaking are involved, these times have been added on separately: eg, 15 minutes + 30 minutes to marinate.

10 minutes

Cooking time. Cooking times do not include the cooking of side dishes or accompaniments served with the main dishes.

chicken & barley stew
page 70

chicken pinwheels with
blue cheese & herbs, page 92

Making soup at home is quick, easy, and satisfying, and an economical way of using leftover chicken. The soups in this section reflect the delightful flavors of international cuisine, such as the Thai Chicken Soup, which evokes the unforgettable flavors of Thailand, and the delicious Scottish Cock-a-Leekie, a comforting soup for cold days and nights. This section also features some very tempting appetizers, such as succulent Bread-Crumbed Chicken Morsels, and sumptuous Chicken Livers in Red Wine & Thyme.

soups & appetizers

thai chicken soup

very easy   serves 4

15–20
minutes   30 minutes

ingredients

1 tbsp sesame oil or chili oil
2 garlic cloves, chopped
2 scallions, trimmed and sliced
1 leek, trimmed and finely sliced
1 tbsp grated fresh gingerroot
1 red chile, seeded and finely chopped
12 oz/350 g skinless chicken breasts,
    cut into strips

scant 3½ cups chicken bouillon
2 tbsp rice wine
1 tbsp chopped lemongrass
6 kaffir lime leaves, finely shredded
7 oz/200 g fine egg noodles
salt and pepper

Heat the oil in a wok or large pan. Add the garlic and cook over medium heat, stirring, for 1 minute, then add the scallions, leek, gingerroot, and chile and cook, stirring, for another 3 minutes. Add the chicken strips, bouillon, and rice wine, bring to a boil, and simmer for 20 minutes. Stir in the lemongrass and lime leaves.

Bring a separate pan of water to a boil and add the noodles. Cook for 3 minutes, drain well, then add them to the soup. Season with salt and pepper.
Cook for another 2 minutes. Remove from the heat, ladle into individual bowls, and serve hot.

cilantro chicken soup

very easy   serves 4

15–20 minutes   30 minutes

ingredients

1 tbsp sunflower oil
1 garlic clove, finely chopped
6 shallots, chopped
2 scallions, trimmed and finely sliced
1 tbsp grated fresh gingerroot
1 small red chile, seeded and
    finely chopped
10½ oz/300 g skinless chicken breasts,
    cut into strips

4 cups chicken bouillon
3 oz/85 g fresh oyster mushrooms, sliced
1¼ oz/35 g fresh cilantro leaves, chopped
1 tbsp Thai fish sauce
1 tbsp grated lemon zest
2 tbsp lemon juice
1 tbsp chopped fresh lemongrass
salt and pepper
1¾ cups bean sprouts

Heat the sunflower oil in a wok or large pan. Add the garlic and cook over medium heat, stirring, for 1 minute, then add the shallots, scallions, gingerroot, and chile and cook, stirring, for another 3 minutes. Add the chicken strips, bouillon, mushrooms, and cilantro, and bring to a boil. Lower the heat and stir in the fish sauce and the lemon zest and juice. Simmer for 20 minutes.

Stir in the lemongrass and season with salt and pepper. Cook for about 2 minutes, then add the bean sprouts. Cook for another minute, then remove from the heat, ladle into individual bowls, and serve hot.

cock-a-leekie soup

easy   serves 4

15–20   3 hours
minutes

ingredients

4 leeks, trimmed
1 small whole chicken, ready
  for boiling
4 strips lean bacon
2 tbsp chopped fresh parsley
1 tbsp chopped fresh thyme
1 bay leaf

6½ cups water
salt and pepper
generous ¾ cup heavy cream

GARNISH
12 whole cooked prunes, pitted
1 tbsp chopped fresh parsley

Chop the leeks and put them into a large pot with the chicken, bacon, herbs, and water. Season with salt and pepper. Bring to a boil, then lower the heat, cover the pan, and simmer for about 2¾ hours, topping up the water level when necessary.

Remove from the heat and strain the soup into a large bowl. Remove the flesh from the chicken, cut into strips and add to the bowl. Discard the carcass. Cut the bacon into strips and add to the bowl with the chicken meat. Return the soup to the pot and add the rest of the leeks. Bring back to a boil, then lower the heat and simmer for 15 minutes. Stir in the cream and warm through gently, then remove from the heat and ladle into individual bowls. Garnish with whole prunes and chopped parsley and serve.

chicken & shrimp laksa

very easy   serves 4

15 minutes   30 minutes

ingredients

1 tbsp sesame oil
3 scallions, trimmed and sliced
2 tbsp Thai red curry paste
1 tbsp cornstarch
2 tbsp coconut milk
scant 2 cups chicken bouillon
11½ oz/325 g skinless chicken breasts,
   cut into strips

2 tbsp chopped fresh cilantro
salt and pepper
8 oz/225 g vermicelli
7 oz/200 g cooked shrimp, peeled
1½ cups evaporated milk
1¾ cups bean sprouts

chopped fresh cilantro, to garnish

Heat the oil in a wok or large pan. Add the scallions and cook, stirring, for 2 minutes. Add the curry paste and cook for another minute. Stir in the cornstarch and coconut milk, then add the bouillon, chicken strips, and cilantro. Season with salt and pepper. Bring to a boil, then lower the heat, cover the pan, and simmer for 20 minutes.

About halfway through the cooking time, bring a pan of lightly salted water to a boil and add the vermicelli. Cook over medium heat for about 10 minutes if using dried pasta, or 4 minutes if using fresh (check the instructions on the package), until tender but still firm to the bite. Remove from the heat, drain, and divide between 4 soup bowls. Add the shrimp and evaporated milk to the chicken mixture and cook for 1 minute. Add the bean sprouts, cook for another minute, then remove from the heat. Ladle the mixture over the vermicelli, garnish with cilantro, and serve hot.

bread-crumbed chicken morsels

very easy   serves 4

20 minutes   30 minutes

1¾ cups fresh white or whole-wheat
   bread crumbs
3 tbsp grated romano cheese
1 tbsp dried mixed herbs
salt and pepper
1 egg
4 skinless chicken breasts, cut into
   thick strips

TARTARE SAUCE
generous ¾ cup mayonnaise

1 tbsp lemon juice
2 tbsp chopped fresh chives
1 garlic clove, finely chopped
1 tbsp capers, chopped
2 shallots, finely chopped
1¾ oz/50 g dill pickles, chopped
6 black olives, pitted and finely chopped

wedges of lemon, to garnish

fresh mixed salad greens, to serve

Preheat the oven to 400°F/200°C. Put the bread crumbs into a large, shallow
bowl. Add the romano cheese and mixed herbs and season well with salt and
pepper. Mix together well. Beat the egg in a separate bowl. Dip the chicken strips
into the beaten egg, then coat them in the bread crumb mixture. Arrange on a
cookie sheet, then transfer to the preheated oven. Bake for 30 minutes until golden.

Meanwhile, to make the tartare sauce, put the mayonnaise into a bowl and stir in
the lemon juice and chives. Add the garlic, capers, shallots, dill pickles, and olives
and mix together well.

Arrange the mixed salad greens on a large serving platter. Remove the chicken
from the oven and arrange over the salad greens. Garnish with lemon wedges and
serve with the tartare sauce.

chicken crostini

very easy   serves 4

15 minutes 10 minutes

12 slices French bread or rustic bread
4 tbsp olive oil
2 garlic cloves, chopped
2 tbsp finely chopped fresh oregano
salt and pepper
3½ oz/100 g cold roast chicken, cut into
   small, thin slices

4 tomatoes, sliced
12 thin slices of goat cheese
12 black olives, pitted and chopped
fresh red and green lettuce leaves,
   to serve

Preheat the oven to 350°F/180°C and the broiler to medium. Put the bread under the preheated broiler and lightly toast on both sides. Meanwhile, pour the olive oil into a bowl and add the garlic and oregano. Season with salt and pepper and mix well. Remove the toasted bread slices from the broiler and brush them on one side only with the oil mixture.

Place the bread slices, oiled sides up, on a cookie sheet. Put some sliced chicken on top of each one, followed by a slice of tomato. Divide the slices of goat cheese between them, then top with the chopped olives. Drizzle over the remaining oil mixture and transfer to the preheated oven. Bake for about 5 minutes, or until the cheese is golden and starting to melt. Remove from the oven and serve on a bed of fresh red and green lettuce leaves.

spicy chicken dippers

very easy   serves 4

15–20   30 minutes
minutes

ingredients

1¾ cups fresh white or
    whole-wheat bread crumbs
3 tbsp freshly grated Parmesan cheese
1 tsp chili powder
salt and pepper
1 egg
4 skinless chicken breasts, cut into
    thick strips

SPICY TOMATO DIP
3½ oz/100 g cream cheese

1 tbsp tomato paste
1 small red chili, seeded and
    finely chopped
1 large tomato, seeded and
    finely chopped
2 tbsp finely chopped peeled cucumber
cherry tomatoes, halved, to garnish

TO SERVE
fresh salad greens
celery and carrots, cut into thick sticks

Preheat the oven to 400°F/200°C. Put the bread crumbs into a large, shallow bowl. Add the Parmesan and chili powder, season with salt and pepper, and mix well. Beat the egg in a separate bowl. Dip the chicken strips into the egg, then coat them in the bread crumb mixture. Arrange on a cookie sheet and transfer to the preheated oven. Bake for 30 minutes until golden.

Meanwhile, to make the dip, put the cream cheese into a bowl and stir in the tomato paste. Add the chili, tomato, and cucumber and mix together well.

Arrange the salad greens on a large serving platter. Remove the chicken from the oven and arrange over the salad greens. Garnish with cherry tomatoes and serve with the celery and carrot sticks and the spicy tomato dip.

chicken livers in red wine & thyme

extremely
easy

serves 4

10 minutes   5 minutes

ingredients

9 oz/250 g fresh chicken livers
3 tbsp lemon-flavored oil
2 garlic cloves, finely chopped
4 tbsp red wine
1 tbsp chopped fresh thyme
salt and pepper
sprigs of fresh thyme, to garnish

TO SERVE
arugula leaves
fresh crusty bread

Rinse the chicken livers under cold running water and pat dry with paper towels.
Heat the lemon-flavored oil in a skillet. Add the garlic and cook, stirring, over
medium heat for 2 minutes. Add the chicken livers, wine, and thyme. Season with
salt and pepper and cook for 3 minutes.

Meanwhile, arrange the arugula leaves on a large serving platter. Remove the
pan from the heat and spoon the chicken livers over the bed of arugula.
Pour over the cooking juices, then garnish with sprigs of fresh thyme and serve
with fresh crusty bread.

This section is crammed with delicious salads, snacks, and light meals to tempt the taste buds. From Chicken, Cheese & Arugula salad to mouthwatering Buttered Chicken Parcels, and from Chicken with Creamy Spaghetti to Chicken in Cranberry & Red Wine Sauce, these dishes will be irresistible. In fact, if you find that there is never enough of these lighter dishes to go round, why not serve them as an entrée? Just add some substantial accompaniments, such as crusty bread or freshly cooked rice or potatoes, and you will have a complete and satisfying meal.

salads & light meals

thai-style chicken salad

extremely easy

serves 4

15 minutes

20 minutes

14 oz/400 g small new potatoes, scrubbed and cut in half, lengthwise
7 oz/200 g baby corn cobs, sliced
1½ cups bean sprouts
3 scallions, trimmed and sliced
4 cooked, skinless chicken breasts, sliced
1 tbsp chopped lemongrass
2 tbsp chopped fresh cilantro
salt and pepper

DRESSING
6 tbsp chili oil or sesame oil
2 tbsp lime juice
1 tbsp light soy sauce
1 tbsp chopped fresh cilantro
1 small, red chili, seeded and finely chopped

GARNISH
wedges of lime
fresh cilantro leaves

Bring two pans of water to the boil. Put the potatoes into one pan and cook for 15 minutes until tender. Put the corn cobs into the other pan and cook for 5 minutes until tender. Drain the potatoes and corn cobs well and let cool.

When the vegetables are cool, transfer them into a large serving dish. Add the bean sprouts, scallions, chicken, lemongrass, and cilantro and season with salt and pepper.

To make the dressing, put all the ingredients into a screw-top jar and shake well. Alternatively, put them into a bowl and mix together well. Drizzle the dressing over the salad and garnish with lime wedges and cilantro leaves. Serve at once.

chicken, cheese & arugula salad

extremely
easy

serves 4

15 minutes

ingredients

5½ oz/150 g arugula leaves
2 celery stalks, trimmed and sliced
½ cucumber, sliced
2 scallions, trimmed and sliced
2 tbsp chopped fresh parsley
1 oz/25 g walnut pieces
12 oz/350 g boneless roast chicken, sliced
4½ oz/125 g Stilton cheese, cubed

handful of seedless red grapes,
    cut in half (optional)
salt and pepper

DRESSING
2 tbsp olive oil
1 tbsp sherry vinegar
1 tsp Dijon mustard
1 tbsp chopped mixed herbs

Wash the arugula leaves, pat dry with paper towels, and put them into a large salad bowl. Add the celery, cucumber, scallions, parsley, and walnuts and mix together well. Transfer onto a large serving platter. Arrange the chicken slices over the salad, then scatter over the cheese. Add the red grapes, if using. Season well with salt and pepper.

To make the dressing, put all the ingredients into a screw-top jar and shake well. Alternatively, put them into a bowl and mix together well. Drizzle the dressing over the salad and serve.

sage & onion drumsticks

very easy   serves 4

25 minutes   55 minutes

ingredients

6 tbsp butter

1 onion, finely chopped

1 garlic clove, finely chopped

2½ cups fresh white or
    whole-wheat bread crumbs

2 tbsp finely chopped fresh sage

1 tbsp lemon juice

salt and pepper

8 large chicken drumsticks

2 eggs, beaten

3 tbsp vegetable oil

GARNISH

wedges of lemon

sprigs of fresh flatleaf parsley

fresh salad greens, to serve

Preheat the oven to 400°F/200°C. Melt the butter in a skillet over medium heat. Add the onion and garlic and cook, stirring, for 3 minutes. Remove from the heat and stir in the bread crumbs, sage, and lemon juice. Season well with salt and pepper. Transfer to a large bowl.

Rinse the drumsticks and pat dry with paper towels. Turn the drumsticks in the beaten egg, then coat them in the sage and onion mixture by pressing it around them. Arrange them in a shallow roasting pan, drizzle over the oil, then roast them in the preheated oven for about 50 minutes until golden and crispy and cooked right through. If they start to brown too quickly, cover the roasting pan with foil. Remove from the oven and pile onto a serving platter. Garnish with lemon wedges and sprigs of fresh flatleaf parsley and serve with salad. Alternatively, to serve cold, let cool, cover with plastic wrap, and refrigerate until required.

buttered chicken parcels

easy   serves 4

15–20
minutes +
10 minutes
to cool

35 minutes

ingredients

4 tbsp butter
4 shallots, finely chopped
10½ oz/300 g frozen spinach, thawed
1 lb/450 g blue cheese, such as
  Stilton, crumbled
1 egg, lightly beaten
1 tbsp chopped fresh chives
1 tbsp chopped fresh oregano

pepper
4 large, skinless chicken breasts
8 slices prosciutto

fresh chives, to garnish

baby spinach leaves, to serve

Melt half of the butter in a skillet over medium heat. Add the shallots and cook, stirring, for 4 minutes. Remove from the heat and let cool for 10 minutes.

Preheat the oven to 350°F/180°C. Using your hands, squeeze out as much moisture from the thawed spinach as possible. Transfer the spinach into a large bowl, add the shallots, cheese, egg, herbs, and seasoning. Mix together well.

Halve each chicken breast and pound lightly to flatten each piece. Spoon some cheese mixture into the center of each piece, then roll them up. Wrap each roll in a slice of prosciutto and secure with a toothpick. Transfer to a roasting dish and dot with the remaining butter. Bake in the preheated oven for 30 minutes until golden.

Divide the baby spinach leaves between 4 serving plates. Remove the chicken from the oven and place 2 chicken rolls on each bed of spinach. Garnish with fresh chives and serve.

crispy coated chicken breasts

ingredients

easy   serves 4

15–20 minutes   45–55 minutes

SWEET POTATO WEDGES
4 large sweet potatoes, peeled and
   cut into wedges
4 tbsp vegetable oil
1 tsp chili powder
1¾ oz/50 g hazelnuts, toasted and ground
3 tbsp dried white or whole-wheat
   bread crumbs
2 tbsp freshly grated romano cheese

1 tbsp chopped fresh parsley
salt and pepper
4 skinless chicken breasts
1 egg, beaten
4 tbsp vegetable oil

sprigs of fresh flatleaf parsley, to garnish

wedges of lemon, to serve

Preheat the oven to 400°F/200°C. To make the potato wedges, bring a large pan of water to a boil. Add the potatoes and cook over medium heat for 5 minutes. Drain well. Pour 2 tablespoons of the oil into a large bowl and stir in the chili powder. Add the potatoes and turn in the mixture until coated. Transfer to a cookie sheet, drizzle over the remaining oil, and bake for 35–40 minutes, turning frequently, until golden and cooked through.

About 15 minutes before the end of the cooking time, put the hazelnuts, bread crumbs, cheese, and parsley into a bowl, season, and mix. Dip the chicken breasts into the egg, then coat in the bread crumb mixture. Heat the oil in a skillet. Add the chicken and cook over medium heat for 3–4 minutes on each side until golden. Lift out and drain on paper towels. Remove the potatoes from the oven, divide between 4 serving plates, and add a chicken breast to each. Garnish with parsley and serve with lemon wedges.

chicken kiev

easy   serves 4

20 minutes   5 minutes

ingredients

4 tbsp butter, softened
1 garlic clove, finely chopped
1 tbsp finely chopped fresh parsley
1 tbsp finely chopped fresh oregano
salt and pepper
4 skinless chicken breasts
generous 1 cup vegetable oil,
    for deep-frying
1¾ cups fresh white or
    whole-wheat bread crumbs

3 tbsp freshly grated Parmesan cheese
1 egg, beaten

GARNISH
slices of lemon
sprigs of fresh flatleaf parsley

TO SERVE
freshly cooked new potatoes
selection of cooked vegetables

Put the butter and garlic into a bowl and mix together well. Stir in the chopped herbs and season well with salt and pepper. Pound the chicken breasts to flatten them, then put a tablespoon of herb butter in the center of each one. Fold in the sides to enclose the butter, then secure with toothpicks.

Pour oil into a pan to a depth that will cover the chicken parcels. Heat until very hot. Meanwhile, combine the bread crumbs and grated Parmesan on a plate. Dip the chicken parcels into the beaten egg, then coat in the bread crumb mixture. Transfer the chicken to the hot oil and cook for 5 minutes, or until cooked through. Lift out the chicken and drain on paper towels. Divide the chicken between 4 serving plates, garnish with lemon slices and sprigs of fresh flatleaf parsley, and serve with new potatoes and a selection of vegetables.

chicken & peanut stir-fry

very easy   serves 4

15 minutes   8–9 minutes

ingredients

2 tbsp peanut oil
1 garlic clove, chopped
3 scallions, trimmed and sliced
4 skinless chicken breasts,
    cut into bite-size chunks
1 tbsp grated fresh gingerroot
½ tsp chili powder
5½ oz/150 g sugar snap peas, trimmed

4½ oz/125 g baby corn cobs
2 tbsp smooth peanut butter
1 tbsp light soy sauce

TO SERVE
freshly cooked brown or white rice
fresh green and red salad leaves

Heat the oil in a preheated wok or large skillet. Add the garlic and scallions and stir-fry over medium-high heat for 1 minute. Add the chicken pieces, gingerroot, and chili powder and stir-fry for 4 minutes. Add the sugar snap peas and baby corn cobs and cook for 2 minutes.

In a bowl, mix together the peanut butter and soy sauce, then add it to the wok. Stir-fry for another minute. Remove from the heat, pile onto 4 serving plates, and serve with freshly cooked rice.

five-spice chicken with vegetables

very easy   serves 4

15 minutes   9–10
minutes

ingredients

2 tbsp sesame oil
1 garlic clove, chopped
3 scallions, trimmed and sliced
1 tbsp cornstarch
2 tbsp rice wine
4 skinless chicken breasts, cut into strips
1 tbsp Chinese five-spice powder
1 tbsp grated fresh gingerroot

½ cup chicken bouillon
3½ oz/100 g baby corn cobs, sliced
3 cups bean sprouts

finely chopped scallions, to
    garnish, optional

freshly cooked jasmine rice, to serve

Heat the oil in a preheated wok or large skillet. Add the garlic and scallions and stir-fry over medium-high heat for 1 minute.

In a bowl, mix together the cornstarch and rice wine, then add the mixture to the pan. Stir-fry for 1 minute, then add the chicken, five-spice powder, gingerroot, and chicken bouillon and cook for another 4 minutes. Add the corn cobs and cook for 2 minutes, then add the bean sprouts and cook for another minute.

Remove from the heat, garnish with chopped scallions, if using, and serve with freshly cooked jasmine rice.

chicken with creamy spaghetti

very easy   serves 4

10–15 minutes + 3 hours to marinate   8–16 minutes

ingredients

MARINADE
2 tbsp olive oil
6 tbsp white wine
1 garlic clove, chopped
1 tbsp chopped fresh thyme
1 tbsp chopped fresh rosemary
4 skinless chicken breasts, cut into strips
1 lb/450 g spaghetti

salt and pepper
2 tbsp olive oil
6 tbsp sour cream
1 tbsp chopped fresh thyme

GARNISH
freshly grated Parmesan cheese
sprigs of fresh rosemary

To make the marinade, put all the ingredients into a large, shallow, glass dish and mix together well. Add the chicken and coat in the marinade. Cover with plastic wrap and refrigerate for 3 hours.

Bring a pan of lightly salted water to a boil and add the spaghetti. Cook over medium heat for about 10 minutes if using dried pasta, or 4 minutes if using fresh (check the instructions on the package), until tender but still firm to the bite. Meanwhile, lift the chicken out of the marinade, drain, and season. Discard the marinade. Heat the oil in a skillet, add the chicken, and cook over medium heat for 2–3 minutes on each side, or until cooked through.

In a bowl, mix the sour cream with the thyme. Drain the spaghetti and mix with half of the sour cream. Pile the spaghetti onto a large serving platter, then top with the chicken. Pour over the remaining sour cream, scatter over the Parmesan, garnish with rosemary sprigs, and serve.

lemon chicken with rice

very easy　　serves 4

10–15
minutes +
3 hours to
marinate　　10 minutes

ingredients

4 skinless chicken breasts, cut into
　　bite-size chunks
salt and pepper
4 tbsp butter
1 garlic clove, chopped
1 onion, thinly sliced
juice and grated zest of 1 lemon
½ cup chicken bouillon

MARINADE
juice and grated zest of 1 lemon
2 garlic cloves, chopped

3 tbsp lemon oil
6 tbsp white wine
1 tbsp chopped fresh cilantro

GARNISH
toasted slivered almonds
fresh cilantro leaves

TO SERVE
freshly cooked rice
selection of freshly cooked vegetables

To make the marinade, put all the ingredients into a large, shallow, glass dish
and mix together well. Add the chicken and coat in the marinade. Cover with
plastic wrap and refrigerate for 3 hours.

Lift out the chicken, drain well, and season. Discard the marinade. Heat the
butter in a skillet, add the garlic and onion, and cook over low heat, stirring,
for 2 minutes. Add the lemon juice and zest, bouillon, and chicken and bring to a
boil. Lower the heat to medium and cook for 7–8 minutes, or until cooked through.

Arrange the cooked rice on a large serving platter. Remove the pan from the heat
and place the chicken mixture over the rice. Scatter over the almonds and cilantro
leaves. Serve with a selection of freshly cooked vegetables.

chicken in cranberry & red wine sauce

easy   serves 4

20 minutes   1 hour 25 minutes

ingredients

1¼ cups chicken bouillon
4 skinless, boneless chicken breasts
1 bay leaf
salt and pepper

LEMON POTATOES
1 lb 5 oz/600 g small new potatoes,
    scrubbed
2 garlic cloves, chopped
3 tbsp olive oil

juice of ½ lemon
1 tbsp chopped fresh thyme
salt and pepper

CRANBERRY & RED WINE SAUCE
1¾ cups fresh cranberries
½ cup superfine sugar
1¼ cups red wine

sprigs of fresh thyme, to garnish

Preheat the oven to 400°F/200°C. Arrange the potatoes in a roasting pan.
Put the garlic, oil, lemon juice, and chopped thyme into a bowl, season, and mix
well. Pour the mixture over the potatoes and turn the potatoes until thoroughly
coated. Roast in the preheated oven for 50 minutes, basting occasionally, until
golden brown and tender.

Halfway through the cooking time, pour the bouillon into a pan and bring to a boil.
Add the chicken and bay leaf, reduce the heat, and simmer for about 20 minutes,
until cooked through. To make the sauce, put all the ingredients into a pan and
bring to a boil. Reduce the heat and simmer, stirring occasionally, for 15 minutes,
until thickened. Lift out the chicken and discard the bay leaf. Slice the chicken
and arrange on 4 serving plates. Remove the potatoes from the oven and divide
between the plates. Spoon over the sauce, garnish with thyme, and serve.

sweet & sour chicken

very easy   serves 4

15 minutes   40–45 minutes

ingredients

4 skinless chicken breasts
salt and pepper
½ cup all-purpose flour
2 tbsp olive oil
2 large garlic cloves, chopped
1 bay leaf
1 tbsp grated fresh gingerroot
1 tbsp chopped fresh lemongrass
4 tbsp sherry vinegar
5 tbsp rice wine or sherry
1 tbsp honey

1 tsp chili powder
½ cup orange juice
4 tbsp lime juice

TO GARNISH
toasted slivered almonds
wedges of lime

TO SERVE
sautéed sliced potatoes
carrots, cut into sticks and freshly cooked

Season the chicken breasts on both sides with salt and pepper, then roll them in the flour until coated. Heat the olive oil in a large skillet. Add the garlic and cook, stirring, over medium heat for 1 minute. Add the chicken, bay leaf, gingerroot, and lemongrass and cook for 2 minutes on each side.

Add the vinegar, rice wine, and honey, bring to a boil, then lower the heat and simmer, stirring occasionally, for 10 minutes. Add the chili powder, then stir in the orange juice and lime juice. Simmer for another 10 minutes. Using a perforated spoon, lift out the chicken and set aside. Strain and reserve the liquid and discard the bay leaf, then return the liquid to the pan with the chicken. Simmer for another 15–20 minutes.

Remove from the heat and transfer to individual serving plates. Garnish with toasted slivered almonds and lime wedges, and serve with sautéed sliced potatoes and freshly cooked carrots.

stuffed chicken breasts with herbs

easy   serves 4

15 minutes   35 minutes

ingredients

4 tbsp butter
1 onion, finely chopped
4 strips smoked lean bacon, chopped
1 lb/450 g Swiss cheese, grated
1 egg, lightly beaten
1 tbsp chopped fresh sage
2 tbsp chopped fresh basil
salt and pepper
4 large, skinless chicken breasts

TO GARNISH
toasted pine nuts
sprigs of fresh basil

freshly cooked paglia e fieno,
    or other pasta ribbons, to serve

Preheat the oven to 350°F/180°C. Melt half of the butter in a skillet over medium heat. Add the onion and cook, stirring, for 2 minutes. Add the bacon and cook for another 2 minutes. Remove from the heat and transfer to a large bowl. Add the cheese, egg, and herbs to the bowl. Season with salt and pepper and mix together well.

Halve each chicken breast and pound lightly to flatten each piece. Spoon some bacon mixture into the center of each piece, roll up, and secure with toothpicks. Transfer to a large roasting dish and dot with the remaining butter. Bake in the preheated oven for 30 minutes until golden.

Divide the freshly cooked pasta between 4 serving plates. Remove the chicken from the oven and place 2 chicken rolls on top of each bed of pasta. Garnish with toasted pine nuts and sprigs of fresh basil and serve.

Chicken is popular in cooking all over the world. This section presents a spectacular array of exciting and satisfying dishes from different countries, such as Italian Pesto Chicken, and Coq au Vin from France. There is also a Fiery Chicken Vindaloo, which takes its inspiration from India. And what could demonstrate chicken's marvelous versatility better than Mexican Chicken with Chile Chocolate Sauce? Mexican cooks have been pairing rich chocolate with hot chiles for centuries, and the flavor of chicken complements this combination perfectly.

entrées

roast chicken with hazelnut stuffing

easy · serves 4

15 minutes
+ 10 minutes
to rest · 1 hour
45 minutes

ingredients

3 tbsp butter, softened
1 garlic clove, finely chopped
3 tbsp finely chopped toasted hazelnuts
1 tbsp grated lemon zest
1 tbsp chopped fresh flatleaf parsley
salt and pepper
1 medium oven-ready chicken,
   about 4 lb/1.8 kg
1 lemon, cut into fourths
1 tbsp olive oil
generous 1¾ cups sherry

1 tsp ground cumin
1 heaping tsp cornstarch

TO GARNISH
slices of lemon
sprigs of fresh flatleaf parsley

TO SERVE
roast potatoes
selection of freshly cooked vegetables

Preheat the oven to 375°F/190°C. Mix 1 tablespoon of the butter with the garlic, hazelnuts, lemon zest, and parsley. Season well. Loosen the chicken skin from the breast without breaking it. Push the butter mixture evenly between the skin and breast meat. Put the lemon wedges inside the body cavity.

Pour the olive oil into a roasting pan. Put the chicken in it. Pour over the sherry, season, rub the skin with cumin, and dot with the remaining butter. Roast for 1 hour 40 minutes, basting occasionally, until cooked through. Check it is cooked by inserting a knife into the thick part of a thigh—the juices should run clear. Lift out onto a serving plate to rest for 10 minutes. Mix the cornstarch with 2 tablespoons of water, then stir into the juices in the pan. Transfer to the stove. Stir over low heat until thickened. Add more water if necessary. Garnish the chicken with lemon slices and parsley. Serve with potatoes, vegetables, and the cooking sauce.

honey-glazed chicken

easy   serves 4

15 minutes   1 hour
+ 10 minutes   45 minutes
to rest

ingredients

3 tbsp clear honey

½ tsp salt

1 tsp powdered mustard

1 tbsp light soy sauce

1 tbsp olive oil

1 medium oven-ready chicken,
  about 4 lb/1.8 kg

1 orange, cut into fourths

⅔ cup chicken bouillon

1 tsp cornstarch

⅔ cup red wine

⅔ cup light cream

seedless red grapes, cut in half,
  to garnish

freshly cooked white rice and
  wild rice, to serve

Preheat the oven to 375°F/190°C. Put the honey, salt, mustard, and soy sauce into a bowl and mix well. Pour the olive oil into a roasting pan and place the chicken in it. Put the orange wedges inside the body cavity. Pour over the bouillon, then spread over the honey mixture. Roast for 1 hour 40 minutes, basting occasionally, until golden and cooked through. To check it is cooked, insert a knife into a thickest part of the thigh-the juices should run clear. Lift out the chicken and let rest for 10 minutes.

Mix the cornstarch with 1–2 tablespoons of water, then stir into the juices in the roasting pan. Transfer to the stove and stir over low heat for 1 minute, then pour in the wine. Bring to a boil, lower the heat, and cook, stirring, for 1 minute. Remove from the heat and stir in the cream. Arrange the cooked mixed rice on a serving platter, then place the chicken on it. Garnish with grapes and serve with the red wine sauce.

herb chicken with white wine & vegetables

easy   serves 4

15 minutes 1 hour
+ 10 minutes 45 minutes
to rest

ingredients

2 garlic cloves, finely chopped
1 tbsp chopped fresh flatleaf parsley
1 tbsp chopped fresh thyme
salt and pepper
1 medium oven-ready chicken,
    about 1.8 kg/4 lb
2 shallots, cut in half
1 lemon, cut into fourths
1 bay leaf

1 tbsp olive oil
1¼ cups white wine
1 tbsp cornstarch
sprigs of fresh thyme, to garnish

TO SERVE
roast potatoes
selection of freshly cooked vegetables
gravy

Preheat the oven to 375°F/190°C. Put the garlic, parsley, and thyme into a bowl and mix well. Season well. Loosen the chicken skin from the breast without breaking it. Push the mixture evenly between the skin and breast meat. Put the shallots, lemon wedges, and bay leaf inside the body cavity.

Pour the oil into a roasting pan and place the chicken in it. Pour over half of the wine. Roast for 1 hour 40 minutes, basting occasionally, until golden and cooked through. Check it is cooked by inserting a knife into the thickest part of a thigh-the juices should run clear. Lift out the chicken and let rest for 10 minutes.

Mix the cornstarch with 1–2 tablespoons of water, then stir into the juices in the pan. Transfer to the stove and stir over low heat for 1 minute. Stir in the remaining wine. Bring to a boil, lower the heat, and cook, stirring, for 1 minute.
Cut the chicken into slices, garnish with thyme, and serve with roast potatoes, vegetables, and gravy.

italian pesto chicken

very easy   serves 4

15–20   30 minutes
minutes

ingredients

PESTO
1 oz/25 g fresh basil, thick stems removed
generous 1¼ cups pine nuts
3 garlic cloves, coarsely chopped
scant ½ cup extra-virgin olive oil
¾ cup freshly grated Parmesan cheese
salt and pepper
4 skinless chicken breasts
8 slices prosciutto
2¾ oz/75 g sun-dried tomatoes in olive oil,
    drained and chopped

2 tbsp extra-virgin olive oil
½ cup white wine
7 oz/200 g canned chopped tomatoes

GARNISH
black olives, pitted and halved
sprigs of fresh basil
freshly cooked linguine, to serve

Preheat the oven to 350°F/180°C. To make the pesto, put all the ingredients into a food processor and season with salt and pepper. Blend for a few seconds until smooth.

Halve each chicken breast and pound lightly to flatten each piece. Spread on one side only with pesto, then top with the prosciutto. Add a tablespoon of sun-dried tomatoes to each one, then roll them up and secure with toothpicks.

Pour the olive oil into a large roasting pan. Arrange the chicken in the pan, then pour over the wine. Add the chopped tomatoes and bake in the preheated oven for 30 minutes.

Stir any remaining pesto into the cooked pasta and arrange on 4 serving plates. Remove the chicken from the oven, discard the toothpicks and slice in half, widthwise. Divide between the plates. Pour over some of the cooking sauce, garnish with black olives and sprigs of basil, and serve.

fiery chicken vindaloo

very easy   serves 4

15 minutes   1 hour
             10 minutes

ingredients

1 tsp ground cumin
1 tsp ground cinnamon
2 tsp mustard powder
1½ tsp ground coriander
1 tsp cayenne pepper
5 tbsp red wine vinegar
1 tsp brown sugar
⅔ cup vegetable oil
8 garlic cloves, crushed
3 red onions, sliced

4 skinless chicken breasts, cut into
   bite-size chunks
2 small red chiles, seeded and chopped
1 lb/450 g potatoes, peeled and chopped
1 lb 12 oz/800 g canned chopped tomatoes
1 tbsp tomato paste
a few drops of red food coloring
salt and pepper
freshly boiled rice, to serve

Put the cumin, cinnamon, mustard, ground coriander, and cayenne pepper into a bowl. Add the vinegar and sugar and mix well.

Heat the oil in a large skillet. Add the garlic and onions and cook, stirring, over medium heat for 5 minutes. Add the chicken and cook for another 3 minutes, then add the chiles, potatoes, chopped tomatoes and tomato paste, and a few drops of red food coloring. Stir in the spice mixture, season generously with salt and pepper, and bring to a boil. Lower the heat, cover the pan, and simmer, stirring occasionally, for 1 hour.

Arrange the cooked rice on a large serving platter. Remove the pan from the heat, spoon the chicken mixture over the rice, and serve.

mexican chicken with chili chocolate sauce

ingredients

very easy   serves 4

15–20
minutes   1 hour

2 tbsp chili oil
1 garlic clove, chopped
4 skinless chicken breasts
1 onion, chopped
1 red bell pepper, skinned, seeded,
   and chopped
1 large tomato, skinned, seeded,
   and chopped
1 small red chili, seeded and chopped
1 tbsp unsweetened cocoa

generous 2 cups chicken bouillon
generous ⅓ cup raisins
scant ½ cup pine nuts
1 tsp ground allspice
1 tsp brown sugar
1¾ oz/50 g semisweet chocolate,
   broken into small pieces
scant ½ cup red wine
juice of ½ orange
freshly cooked rice or potatoes, to serve

Heat the oil in a flameproof casserole. Add the garlic and cook, stirring, over medium heat for 3 minutes. Add the chicken and cook for 3 minutes, then turn over and cook on the other side for another 2 minutes. Lift out the chicken, cut into bite-size chunks, and set aside.

Preheat the oven to 350°F/180°C. Add the onion, red bell pepper, tomato, chili, and unsweetened cocoa to the pan. Cook, stirring, for 5 minutes. Then add the bouillon, raisins, pine nuts, allspice, and sugar and cook for 2 minutes. Return the chicken to the casserole. Add the chocolate and stir until melted, then stir in the red wine and orange juice. Bring to a boil then remove from the heat.

Transfer to the preheated oven and bake for about 40 minutes or until cooked through. Remove from the oven and serve with freshly cooked rice or potatoes.

sweet chicken pie

easy   serves 4

20 minutes
+ 1 hour
to chill   1¼ hours

ingredients

PIE DOUGH
2½ cups all-purpose flour, plus extra
   for dusting
pinch of salt
¾ cup butter, chopped, plus extra
   for greasing
about 6 tbsp cold water
1 cup chicken bouillon
1 lb 9 oz/700 g boneless chicken,
   cut into bite-size chunks
1 egg, lightly beaten

3 tbsp brandy
1 tbsp raisins
1¾ oz/50 g hazelnuts, toasted and ground
½ cup grated colby cheese
1 tsp ground allspice
salt and pepper

TO SERVE
freshly cooked potatoes
selection of freshly cooked vegetables
seedless white grapes, halved, optional

To make the dough, mix the flour and salt in a bowl. Rub in the butter to form fine crumbs. Gradually mix in enough cold water to make a pliable dough. Knead lightly. Wrap in plastic wrap and chill in the refrigerator for 1 hour. Meanwhile, pour the bouillon into a pan and bring to a boil. Lower the heat, add the chicken, and cook for 30 minutes. Remove from the heat, cool for 25 minutes, then transfer to a bowl. Stir in the remaining ingredients. Season.

Preheat the oven to 375°F/190°C. Grease a 9-inch/23-cm pie pan with butter. Remove the dough from the refrigerator. On a floured counter, shape half into a ball, roll out to a thickness of ¼ inch/5 mm, and use it to line the pan. Spoon in the chicken filling, then roll out the remaining dough. Moisten the pie rim with water, cover the pie with the remaining dough, and trim the edges. Cut 2 slits in the top and add dough leaf shapes made from trimmings. Brush with the egg. Bake for 45 minutes. Serve with potatoes, vegetables, and grapes if using.

coq au vin

very easy   serves 4

15 minutes   1 hour
10 minutes

ingredients

2 tbsp butter
8 baby onions
4½ oz/125 g lean bacon,
  coarsely chopped
4 fresh chicken joints
1 garlic clove, finely chopped
12 white mushrooms
1¼ cups red wine

1 bouquet garni
1 tbsp chopped fresh tarragon
salt and pepper
2 tsp cornstarch

sprigs of fresh flatleaf parsley, to garnish

sautéed sliced potatoes, to serve

Melt half of the butter in a large skillet over medium heat. Add the onions and bacon and cook, stirring, for 3 minutes. Lift out the bacon and onions and set aside. Melt the remaining butter in the pan and add the chicken. Cook for 3 minutes, then turn over and cook on the other side for 2 minutes. Drain off any excess chicken fat. Return the bacon and onions to the pan, then add the garlic, mushrooms, red wine, and herbs. Season with salt and pepper. Cook for about 1 hour, or until cooked through. Remove from the heat, lift out the chicken, onions, bacon, and mushrooms, transfer them to a serving platter, and keep warm. Discard the bouquet garni.

Mix the cornstarch with 1–2 tablespoons of water, then stir it into the juices in the pan. Bring to a boil, lower the heat, and cook, stirring, for 1 minute. Pour the sauce over the chicken, garnish with sprigs of parsley, and serve with sautéed sliced potatoes.

chicken & barley stew

very easy   serves 4

15 minutes   1 hour

ingredients

2 tbsp vegetable oil

8 small, skinless chicken thighs

generous 2 cups chicken bouillon

scant ½ cup pearl barley, rinsed
    and drained

7 oz/200 g small new potatoes, scrubbed
    and cut in half, lengthwise

2 large carrots, peeled and sliced

1 leek, trimmed and sliced

2 shallots, sliced

1 tbsp tomato paste

1 bay leaf

1 zucchini, trimmed and sliced

2 tbsp chopped fresh parsley

2 tbsp all-purpose flour

salt and pepper

sprigs of fresh flatleaf parsley, to garnish

fresh crusty bread, to serve

Heat the oil in a large pot over medium heat. Add the chicken and cook for
3 minutes, then turn over and cook on the other side for another 2 minutes.
Add the bouillon, barley, potatoes, carrots, leek, shallots, tomato paste, and the
bay leaf. Bring to a boil, lower the heat, and simmer for 30 minutes. Add the
zucchini and parsley, cover the pan, and cook for another 20 minutes, or until the
chicken is cooked through. Remove the bay leaf and discard.

In a separate bowl, mix the flour with 4 tablespoons of water and stir into a smooth
paste. Add it to the stew and cook, stirring, over low heat for another 5 minutes.
Remove from the heat, ladle into individual serving bowls, and garnish with sprigs
of fresh parsley. Serve with fresh crusty bread.

chicken & vegetable bake

very easy   serves 4

10 minutes   30 minutes

ingredients

FILLING

1¼ cups chicken bouillon

1 lb/450 g boneless chicken, chopped

3½ oz/100 g white mushrooms

1 tbsp butter, for greasing

1 tbsp cornstarch

⅔ cup milk

7 oz/200 g carrots, peeled, blanched,
  and chopped

1 tbsp chopped fresh rosemary

salt and pepper

TOPPING

2 lb/900 g potatoes, peeled, cooked,
  and mashed

1 onion, grated

1 cup grated colby cheese

sprigs of fresh rosemary, to garnish

selection of freshly cooked vegetables,
  to serve

To make the filling, pour the bouillon into a large pan and bring to a boil. Add the chicken and mushrooms, lower the heat, cover the pan, and simmer for 25–30 minutes. Grease a 2-pint/1.2-litre ovenproof pie pan with butter. Remove the pan from the heat. Lift out the chicken and mushrooms and place in the prepared pie pan. Reserve the bouillon.

Preheat the oven to 400°F/200°C. In a bowl, mix the cornstarch with enough of the milk to make a smooth paste, then stir in the remaining milk. Stir into the bouillon. Pour the mixture into the pie pan, add the carrots and rosemary, and season well. To make the topping, put the mashed potatoes into a bowl. Add the grated onion and half of the cheese, and mix well. Spoon the mixture over the chicken filling, level the surface, then scatter over the remaining cheese. Bake for 30 minutes until golden. Remove from the oven, garnish with rosemary, and serve with vegetables.

chicken risotto

easy   serves 4

10–15   45–50
minutes   minutes

ingredients

4 tbsp butter

1 onion, chopped

4½ oz/125 g skinless chicken
   breasts, chopped

12 oz/350 g risotto rice

1 tsp turmeric

salt and pepper

1¼ cups white wine

5 cups hot chicken bouillon

2¾ oz/75 g crimini mushrooms, sliced

1¾ oz/50 g cashews, broken in half

TO GARNISH

shavings of fresh Parmesan cheese

fresh basil leaves

fresh arugula, to serve

Melt the butter in a large pan over medium heat. Add the onion and cook, stirring, for 1 minute. Add the chicken and cook, stirring, for another 5 minutes.

Add the rice and cook, stirring, for 15 minutes. Then add the turmeric, season with salt and pepper, and mix well. Gradually stir in the wine, then stir in the hot bouillon, a ladleful at a time, waiting for each ladleful to be absorbed before stirring in the next. Simmer for 20 minutes, stirring from time to time, until the rice is tender and nearly all of the liquid has been absorbed. If necessary, add a little more bouillon to prevent the risotto from drying out. Stir in the mushrooms and cashews, and cook for another 3 minutes.

Arrange the arugula on 4 individual serving plates. Remove the risotto from the heat and spoon it over the arugula. Scatter over the Parmesan shavings and basil leaves and serve at once.

The versatility of chicken makes it the ideal food for entertaining, and this section presents a delicious range of recipes for barbecues, buffets, and dinner parties. Your guests will find the Barbecued Tandoori Chicken irresistible, while the Chicken Pinwheels with Blue Cheese & Herbs will invite many admiring comments. Children will love the Crispy Chicken Burgers, and the elegant Poached Chicken with Brandy & Cream will linger in the memory long after your guests have eaten it.

entertaining

grilled tandoori chicken

very easy   serves 4

15 minutes   15–20
+ 2 hours   minutes
to marinate

ingredients

MARINADE
scant 2 cups plain yogurt
4 tbsp lime juice
2 garlic cloves, crushed
1 tsp salt
pinch of saffron threads
1 tsp ground coriander
1 tsp ground cumin
1 tsp ground ginger
½ tsp chili powder
pepper

SKEWERS
6 skinless chicken breasts
1 red bell pepper, seeded
1 green bell pepper, seeded
16 baby onions

TO GARNISH
lime wedges
fresh cilantro leaves

freshly steamed or boiled rice, to serve

To make the marinade, put the yogurt, lime juice, garlic, salt, and spices into a large, shallow, nonmetallic (glass or ceramic) bowl, which will not react with acid. Season with plenty of pepper and mix together well.

Cut the chicken and bell peppers into bite-size pieces and thread onto 8 skewers, alternating with the onions. When the skewers are full (leave a small space at either end), put them in the bowl and turn in the marinade until they are coated. Cover with plastic wrap and place in the refrigerator to marinate for at least 2 hours.

Lift the skewers out of the marinade. Grill over hot coals or cook under a hot broiler for 15–20 minutes, or until cooked right through, turning them frequently and basting with the remaining marinade. Remove from the heat, arrange on a bed of freshly cooked rice, garnish with fresh cilantro leaves, and serve.

chicken pitas

very easy   serves 4

15 - 20 minutes + 2 hours to marinate   15–20 minutes

ingredients

4 tbsp lemon juice
2 garlic cloves, crushed
1 tsp dried oregano
1 tbsp honey
1 small red chili, seeded and
   finely chopped
salt and pepper
6 skinless chicken breasts, cut into
   bite-size pieces
4 tomatoes, sliced
1 red onion, sliced

7 oz/200 g kalamata olives, pitted
   and cut in half

DRESSING
1 tbsp lemon juice
15 tbsp extra-virgin olive oil
2 tbsp white wine vinegar
½ tsp sugar
2 tbsp chopped fresh cilantro
fresh cilantro leaves, to garnish
8 small pitas, warmed, to serve

Put the lemon juice, garlic, oregano, honey, and chili into a large, shallow, nonmetallic (glass or ceramic) bowl, which will not react with acid. Season with plenty of salt and pepper and mix well. Add the chicken pieces to the bowl and turn them in the marinade until they are coated. Cover with plastic wrap and place in the refrigerator to marinate for at least 2 hours.

Lift the chicken breasts out of the marinade. Grill over hot coals or cook under a hot broiler for 15–20 minutes, or until cooked right through, turning them frequently and basting with the remaining marinade. While they are cooking, make the dressing. Put all the ingredients into a screw-top jar and shake well, or put them into a bowl and mix together. Put the tomatoes, onion, and olives into a separate bowl and drizzle over the dressing. Divide the salad between 8 split pitas and add the cooked chicken. Garnish with cilantro leaves and serve.

chicken & mushroom kabobs

very easy   serves 4

15 minutes   15–20
+ 2 hours   minutes
to marinate

ingredients

MARINADE
½ cup extra-virgin olive oil
2 garlic cloves, crushed
1 tbsp dried basil
1 tbsp dried thyme
salt and pepper

6 skinless chicken breasts, cut into
   bite-size pieces
16 white mushrooms

8 baby onions
8 cherry tomatoes
sprigs of fresh rosemary, to garnish

TO SERVE
fresh salad greens
chopped cucumber
long sprigs of fresh rosemary to use as
   skewers, optional

To make the marinade, put the oil, garlic, basil, and thyme into a large, shallow bowl. Season with salt and pepper and mix well.

Thread the chicken pieces onto 8 skewers (or rosemary skewers, if using), alternating them with the mushrooms, onions, and cherry tomatoes. When the skewers are full (leave a small space at either end), put them into the bowl, and turn them in the marinade until they are well coated. Cover with plastic wrap and place in the refrigerator to marinate for at least 2 hours.

Lift the skewers out of the marinade. Grill over hot coals or cook under a hot broiler for 15–20 minutes, or until cooked right through, turning them frequently and basting with the remaining marinade. Remove from the heat, arrange the skewers on a bed of fresh salad greens and chopped cucumber, garnish with sprigs of fresh rosemary, and serve.

sweet & sour chicken drumsticks

very easy   serves 4

15 minutes + 2 hours to marinate   15–20 minutes

ingredients

MARINADE
4 tbsp sherry vinegar
2 tbsp light soy sauce
3 garlic cloves, crushed
2 tbsp honey
2 tbsp tomato paste
1 tsp paprika
salt and pepper
8 chicken drumsticks

4 long, red chili, made into flowers
  (see below), to garnish

arugula leaves, to serve

To make the marinade, put the vinegar, soy sauce, garlic, honey, tomato paste, and paprika into a large, shallow, nonmetallic (glass or ceramic) bowl, which will not react with acid. Season with salt and pepper and mix well. Add the chicken drumsticks to the bowl and turn in the marinade until well coated. Cover with plastic wrap and place in the refrigerator to marinate for at least 2 hours. Meanwhile, make the chili flowers. Using a sharp knife, make 6 slits about ½ inch/1 cm in length from the stem end to the tip of each chili. Put them in a bowl of iced water and soak for at least 30 minutes until they have expanded into flower shapes.

Lift the drumsticks out of the marinade. Grill over hot coals or cook under a hot broiler for 15–20 minutes, or until cooked through, turning them frequently and basting with the remaining marinade. Arrange the arugula on a large serving platter and pile the cooked drumsticks on top. Garnish with the chili flowers and serve.

honey-glazed chicken skewers

very easy   serves 4

15 minutes   20–25 minutes

ingredients

6 skinless chicken breasts, cut into bite-size pieces
16 white mushrooms
3 red onions, cut into bite-size pieces
2 red bell peppers, seeded and cut into bite-size pieces
2 zucchini, trimmed and cut into bite-size pieces

HONEY GLAZE
2 tbsp white wine vinegar
¾ cup honey
1 tbsp prepared mustard
1 tbsp soy sauce
2 tbsp cornstarch

fresh flatleaf parsley, to garnish

mixture of freshly cooked white rice and wild rice, to serve

Thread the chicken pieces onto 8 skewers, alternating with the mushrooms, onions, red bell peppers, and zucchini (leave a small space at either end).

To make the honey glaze, put the vinegar, honey, mustard, and soy sauce into a small pan and bring to a boil. Meanwhile, in a bowl, mix the cornstarch with enough water to make a smooth paste. When the honey mixture has reached boiling point, lower the heat, stir in the cornstarch mixture, and simmer gently for 1 minute. Remove from the heat.

Brush the honey glaze over the chicken skewers until they are well coated. Grill over hot coals or cook under a hot broiler for 15–20 minutes, or until cooked right through, turning them frequently and basting with the remaining honey glaze. Remove from the heat, arrange on a bed of freshly cooked white rice and wild rice, garnish with fresh parsley, and serve.

mexican citrus chicken

very easy   serves 4

20 minutes   15–20
+ 2 hours   minutes
to marinate

ingredients

MARINADE
1 small red chili, seeded
4 tbsp lime juice
1 tbsp orange juice
4 tbsp extra-virgin olive oil
1 tbsp tequila
4 skinless chicken breasts

CITRUS SALSA
2 tbsp lime juice

2 tbsp orange juice
1 tbsp red wine vinegar
1 garlic clove, crushed
6 tomatoes, coarsely chopped
3 scallions, trimmed and sliced
2 tbsp chopped fresh flatleaf parsley

sprigs of fresh mint, to garnish

8 small flour tortillas, warmed, to serve

To make the marinade, finely chop the chili and put in a large, shallow, nonmetallic (glass or ceramic) bowl with the citrus juices, olive oil, and tequila. Mix well. Halve each chicken breast and pound lightly to tenderize each piece. Add them to the bowl and turn in the marinade until coated. Cover with plastic wrap and place in the refrigerator to marinate for at least 2 hours.

About 30 minutes before the end of the marinating time, make the salsa. Put the lime juice, orange juice, vinegar, and garlic into a large bowl and mix together. Add the tomatoes, scallions, and chopped parsley and toss together until coated. Cover with plastic wrap and let stand for 30 minutes.

Lift the chicken out of the marinade. Grill over hot coals or cook under a hot broiler for 15–20 minutes, or until cooked through, turning frequently and basting with marinade. Divide the chicken and salsa between 8 tortillas, garnish with mint, and serve.

crispy chicken burgers

easy   serves 4

15–20   8–10
minutes +   minutes
30 minutes
to chill

ingredients

4½ cups fresh white or
    whole-wheat bread crumbs
8 oz/225 g cooked chicken meat, chopped
2 eggs
1 onion, coarsely chopped
1 small red chili, seeded and chopped
1 large garlic clove, chopped
1 tbsp grated lemon zest
1 tbsp chopped fresh thyme

1 tbsp chopped fresh parsley
salt and pepper

fresh salad greens, to garnish

TO SERVE
hamburger buns
freshly sliced onion rings and tomatoes,
    cooked or raw

Put 3 cups of the bread crumbs into a food processor with the chicken. Add one of the eggs, then all of the onion, chili, garlic, lemon zest, thyme, and parsley. Season well with salt and pepper, then blend until smooth. Transfer to a bowl, cover with plastic wrap, and refrigerate for 30 minutes.

Remove from the refrigerator and, using your hands, shape the mixture into burgers. Beat the remaining egg, then dip the burgers into the egg and coat with the remaining bread crumbs. Grill over hot coals or cook under a hot broiler for 4–5 minutes on each side, or until cooked right through.

Remove from the heat. Serve with hamburger buns and onion rings and tomatoes, garnished with fresh salad greens.

chicken pinwheels
with blue cheese & herbs

easy   serves 4

15–20 minutes   10–12 minutes

ingredients

2 tbsp pine nuts, lightly toasted
2 tbsp chopped fresh parsley
2 tbsp chopped fresh thyme
1 garlic clove, chopped
1 tbsp grated lemon zest
salt and pepper
4 large, skinless chicken breasts
9 oz/250 g blue cheese, such as Stilton,
   crumbled

GARNISH
twists of lemon
sprigs of fresh thyme

fresh green and red lettuce leaves,
   to serve

Put the pine nuts into a food processor with the parsley, thyme, garlic, and lemon zest. Season with salt and pepper.

Pound the chicken breasts lightly to flatten them. Spread them on one side with the pine nut mixture, then top with the cheese. Roll them up from one short end to the other, so that the filling is enclosed. Wrap the rolls individually in aluminum foil, and seal well. Transfer into a steamer, or a metal colander placed over a pan of boiling water, cover tightly, and steam for 10–12 minutes, or until cooked through.

Arrange the lettuce leaves on a large serving platter. Remove the chicken from the heat, discard the foil, and cut the chicken rolls into slices. Arrange the slices over the lettuce leaves, garnish with twists of lemon and sprigs of thyme, and serve.

poached chicken
with brandy & cream

very easy   serves 4

15 minutes   17–20 minutes

ingredients

1 tbsp butter
1 garlic clove, chopped
2 onions, chopped
scant 2 cups chicken bouillon
1 tbsp chopped fresh tarragon
4 large, skinless chicken breasts
1 large tsp cornstarch
2 tbsp water
3 tbsp brandy

salt and pepper
⅔ cup light cream

GARNISH

sprigs of fresh, flatleaf parsley
seedless white grapes, cut in half

freshly cooked tagliatelle, to serve

Melt the butter in a large pan over low heat. Add the garlic and onion and cook, stirring, for 3 minutes. Add the bouillon and half of the tarragon and bring to a boil. Lower the heat, add the chicken breasts, and cook for 10–12 minutes, or until cooked through.

Lift out the chicken, cut into slices, and keep warm. Strain the chicken bouillon and reserve. Discard the solids. In a separate large, heatproof bowl, mix the cornstarch with 2 tablespoons of water, then gradually stir in the bouillon. Return to the pan and cook gently for 1 minute, then pour in the brandy. Season with salt and pepper and the remaining tarragon. Bring to a boil, lower the heat, and cook, stirring, for 1 minute. Remove from the heat and stir in the cream.

Arrange the cooked pasta on a large serving platter. Arrange the chicken slices over the top and pour over the brandy sauce. Garnish with sprigs of parsley and white grapes and serve.

index